My Mom Works with Technology

Richard Tan

Rosen REAL READERS

Rosen Classroom™
New York

My mom works at this hotel.
It is her job to try to get people
to stay here.

My mom uses technology at her job. Here is my mom in her office.

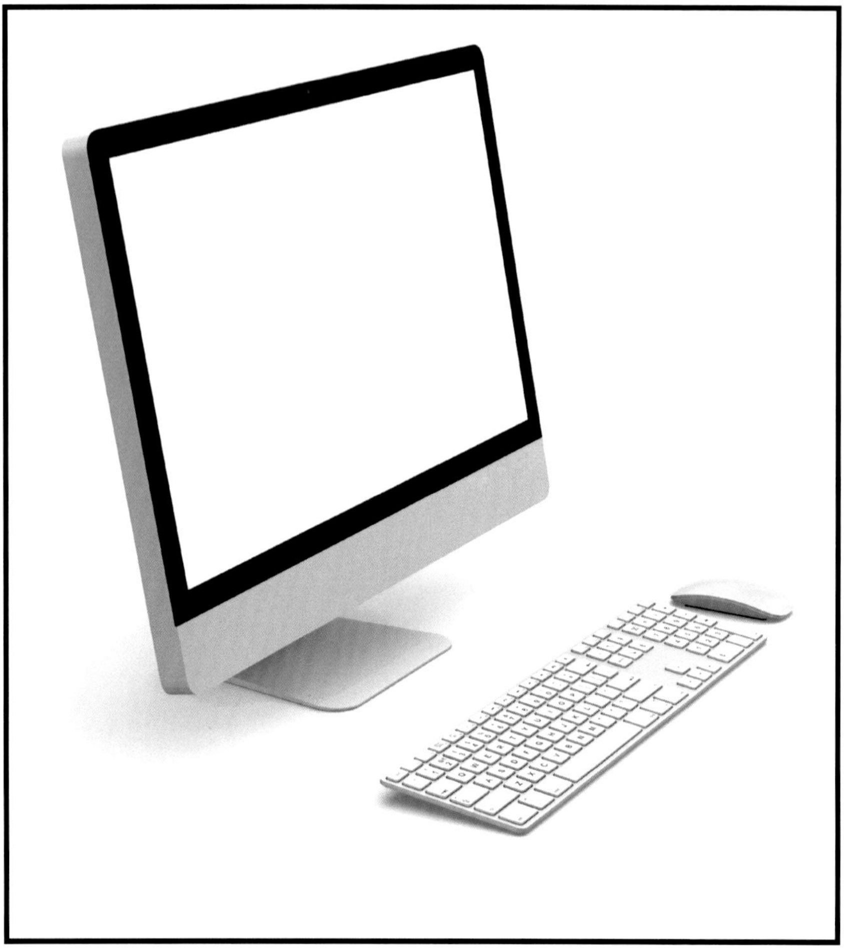

This is my mom's computer.
She uses it every day at work.

My mom gets to work. She turns on her computer and checks her e-mail.

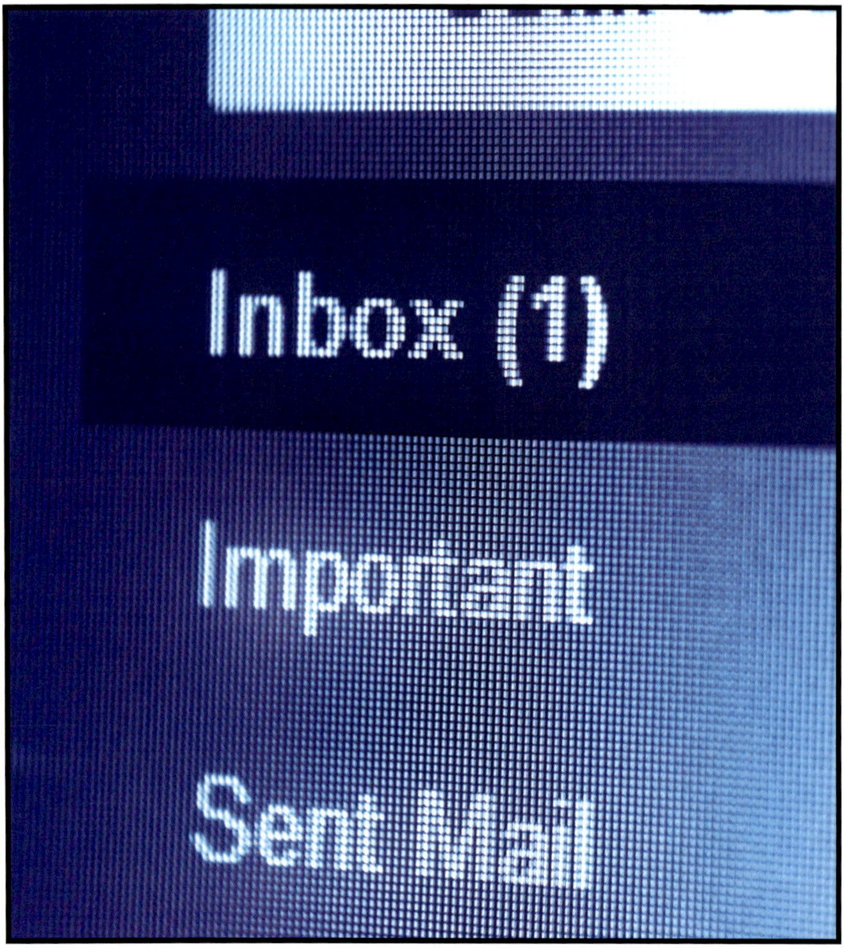

My mom has a new e-mail. It is from her boss. Her boss asks my mom to put together a presentation. The presentation will be about the hotel.

My mom uses special sites on the Internet to research information. She writes down some notes. She writes why people should stay at the hotel.

My mom uses a camera to take photos. She takes photos of the hotel. They will be part of the presentation.

My mom types an invitation to the presentation. She e-mails it to many people.

My mom makes phone calls to more people. She invites them to the presentation too.

It is time for my mom to do her presentation. She shows her presentation with this video projector.

Words to Know

camera

computer

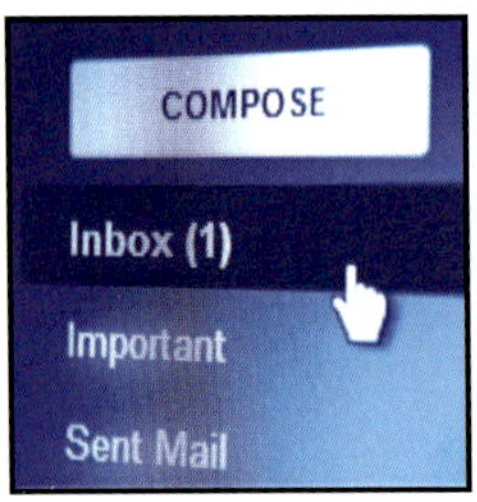

e-mail

hotel

projector

to type